YOU ARE STRONGER THAN YOU THINK

summersdale

YOU ARE STRONGER THAN YOU THINK

Compiled by Luke Forrester

An Hachette UK Company
www.hachette.co.uk

Summersdale Publishers Ltd
Part of Octopus Publishing Group Limited
Carmelite House
50 Victoria Embankment
LONDON
EC4Y 0DZ
UK

www.summersdale.com

Printed and bound in China

ISBN: 978-1-78783-239-8

Substantial discounts on bulk quantities of Summersdale books are available to corporations, professional associations and other organizations. For details contact general enquiries: telephone: +44 (0) 1243 771107 or email: enquiries@summersdale.com.

TO...........................

FROM.........................

The one who falls
and gets up

is stronger

than the one
who never tried.

ROY T. BENNETT

IF YOU'RE TRULY PASSIONATE ABOUT SOMETHING, YOU'LL MAKE IT HAPPEN.

Liam Hemsworth

BE THE BEST YOU CAN BE

I'VE REALIZED THAT
OF ALL THE THINGS
I WANTED, MOST OF
THEM WERE AVAILABLE
TO ME ALL ALONG.

JAMEELA JAMIL

COURAGE IS VERY

important.

LIKE A MUSCLE, IT IS

strengthened

BY USE.

RUTH GORDON

Be **faithful** To THAT WHICH exists Nowhere but in **yourself**.

ANDRÉ GIDE

TODAY I'M CHOOSING CONFIDENCE

THE
RIGHT MENTAL
ATTITUDE WILL
BRING SUCCESS
IN EVERYTHING
YOU UNDERTAKE.

Elbert Hubbard

Worry is a
misuse of the
imagination.

DAN ZADRA

YOU CAN

AND

YOU WILL

With confidence,
you have won
even before you
have started.

MARCUS GARVEY

YOU HAVE TO BE ABLE TO LOVE YOURSELF BECAUSE THAT'S WHEN THINGS FALL INTO PLACE.

Vanessa Hudgens

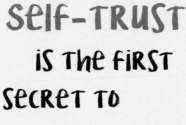

Self-trust is the first secret to success.

RALPH WALDO EMERSON

THERE'S NO

TIME

LIKE THE

PRESENT

WE CAN'T ALLOW
OURSELVES TO BE
FRIGHTENED INTO NOT
LIVING OUR LIVES.
THINGS WILL GET
BETTER WHEN WE
MAKE THEM BETTER.

OPRAH WINFREY

Although the world is full of suffering, it is full also of the overcoming of it.

HELEN KELLER

FEEL
FIERCE

**SPEAK UP.
BELIEVE IN
YOURSELF.
TAKE RISKS.**

Sheryl Sandberg

JUST REMEMBER, YOU
CAN DO ANYTHING
YOU SET YOUR MIND
TO, BUT IT TAKES

action,

perseverance,

AND FACING YOUR

fears.

GILLIAN ANDERSON

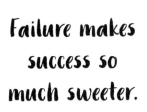

Failure makes
success so
much sweeter.

WILBUR SMITH

CELEBRATE EVERY VICTORY

A LOT OF PEOPLE ARE AFRAID TO SAY WHAT THEY WANT. THAT'S WHY THEY DON'T GET WHAT THEY WANT.

Madonna

I just
breathe
and
believe.

JODI LIVON

CARPE

THAT

DIEM!

INSTEAD OF LETTING
YOUR HARDSHIPS AND
FAILURES DISCOURAGE
OR EXHAUST YOU, LET
THEM INSPIRE YOU.

MICHELLE OBAMA

EVERY MOMENT IS
auspicious.
THERE IS
always some
Magic
IN IT.

AMIT RAY

ONLY THOSE WHO DARE TO FAIL GREATLY CAN EVER ACHIEVE GREATLY.

Robert F. Kennedy

FORGET
— WHAT YOU'RE
NOT AND
LOVE
— WHAT YOU ARE

YOU MUSTN'T
CONFUSE A
single failure
WITH A
final defeat.

F. SCOTT FITZGERALD

Not everything
that is faced can be
changed. But nothing
can be changed
until it is faced.

JAMES BALDWIN

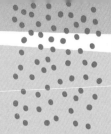

BE
BOLD

SOMETIMES YOU NEED A DOOR SLAMMED IN YOUR FACE BEFORE YOU CAN HEAR OPPORTUNITY KNOCK.

James Geary

We learn
a lot from
the mistakes
of others,
but even
more from
our own.

FAUSTO CERCIGNANI

GREAT DIFFICULTIES
MAY BE SURMOUNTED
BY PATIENCE AND
PERSEVERANCE.

ABIGAIL ADAMS

IT IS ALWAYS DARKEST BEFORE THE

I'M NOT AFRAID OF STORMS, FOR I'M LEARNING how to Sail My Ship.

LOUISA MAY ALCOTT

POWER FOR ME IS "NO"... THAT'S WHEN YOU KNOW YOUR WORTH, WHEN YOU KNOW YOUR VALUE.

Taraji P. Henson

YOU NEED TO BE
SO SURE ABOUT
yourself
AND
your ideas
THAT YOUR
CONFIDENCE
convinces
OTHERS TOO.

RAMI SHAAR

Every flower
blooms at a
different pace.

SUZY KASSEM

TO HAVE STRIVEN, TO HAVE MADE THE EFFORT, TO HAVE BEEN TRUE TO CERTAIN IDEALS – THIS ALONE IS WORTH THE STRUGGLE.

William Osler

NOTHING
CAN
STOP
YOU!

Experience
is not what
happens
to a man; it is
what a man
does with what
happens to him.

ALDOUS HUXLEY

SO MANY OF OUR DREAMS AT FIRST SEEM IMPOSSIBLE. THEN THEY SEEM IMPROBABLE. THEN, WHEN WE SUMMON THE WILL, THEY SOON BECOME INEVITABLE.

CHRISTOPHER REEVE

DON'T STOP UNTIL YOU'RE PROUD

WE NEED

courage.

AMAL CLOONEY

Live out of your
imagination, not
your history.

STEPHEN COVEY

When you

find

your path, you

MUST NOT

be afraid.

PAULO COELHO

A POSITIVE MIND WILL GIVE YOU A POSITIVE LIFE

Where the
willingness
is great, the
difficulties
cannot be great.

NICCOLÒ MACHIAVELLI

FEARLESS IS LIVING IN SPITE OF THOSE THINGS THAT SCARE YOU TO DEATH.

Taylor Swift

ARE YOU READY TO LEAVE YOUR COMFORT ZONE?

THERE ARE MANY WAYS
OF GETTING STRONG.
SOMETIMES TALKING
IS THE BEST WAY.

ANDRE AGASSI

Do your thing and don't care if they like it.

TINA FEY

IF IT DOESN'T CHALLENGE YOU, IT DOESN'T CHANGE YOU.

Fred DeVito

THERE'S **NOTHING** TO FEAR BUT FEAR **ITSELF**

YOU DO
create
YOUR OWN
destiny.

DANIEL RADCLIFFE

Turn your wounds
into wisdom.

OPRAH WINFREY

STOP WORRYING AND START LIVING

I've always believed that you should never, ever give up.

MICHAEL SCHUMACHER

DON'T CRY OVER SPILT
MILK. BY THIS TIME
TOMORROW, IT'LL BE
FREE YOGHURT.

STEPHEN COLBERT

YOUR STRUGGLES develop your STRENGTHS.

ARNOLD SCHWARZENEGGER

BE BIGGER,
BE BETTER,
BE BRAVER

YOU CAN'T
BUILD A
reputation
ON WHAT YOU
ARE GOING
TO DO.

HENRY FORD

Genius is one per cent inspiration,
99 per cent perspiration.

THOMAS EDISON

YOU'RE TOUGHER THAN YOU THINK

THINGS DON'T JUST HAPPEN; THEY ARE MADE TO HAPPEN.

John F. Kennedy

With ordinary
talent,
and extraordinary
perseverance,
all things are
attainable.

THOMAS BUXTON

IF ONE ADVANCES
CONFIDENTLY IN THE
DIRECTION OF HIS
DREAMS... HE WILL
MEET WITH A SUCCESS
UNEXPECTED IN
COMMON HOURS.

HENRY DAVID THOREAU

KEEP
YOUR HEAD
HELD
HIGH

SUCCESSFUL
PEOPLE look
FOR THE
good
IN EVERY
SITUATION.

BRIAN TRACY

How wonderful
IT IS THAT NOBODY
NEED WAIT A
single moment
BEFORE STARTING
TO IMPROVE
the world.

ANNE FRANK

REALIZE YOUR POTENTIAL

Change brings opportunity.

NIDO QUBEIN

I've failed over
and over again
in my life. And
that is why I
succeed.

MICHAEL JORDAN

YOU MUST DO THE THING YOU THINK YOU CANNOT DO.

Eleanor Roosevelt

BE PROUD
OF YOUR
ACHIEVEMENTS

YOU PROBABLY WOULDN'T
WORRY ABOUT WHAT
PEOPLE THINK OF YOU IF
YOU COULD KNOW HOW
SELDOM THEY DO!

OLIN MILLER

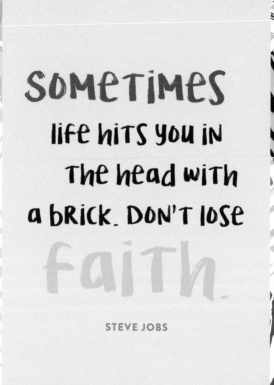

SOMETIMES life hits you in the head with a brick. DON'T lose faith.

STEVE JOBS

WHERE THERE IS

love

AND

inspiration,

I DON'T THINK
YOU CAN
GO WRONG.

ELLA FITZGERALD

THERE'S ALWAYS A WAY.

Britney Spears

You have so
much incredible
potential on
the inside.

JOEL OSTEEN

LIGHT A

FIRE

IN YOUR

BELLY

Life is either a

daring

adventure

or nothing.

HELEN KELLER

PROBLEMS ARE
guidelines,
NOT STOP SIGNS!

ROBERT H. SCHULLER

KEEP
GOING
FORWARD

I CANNOT EMPHASIZE
ENOUGH THE IMPORTANCE
OF A DREAM TO BECOMING
ALL YOU ARE MEANT TO BE.

WADE D. SADLIER

EVERY ADVERSITY
BRINGS WITH IT
the seed
OF AN EQUIVALENT
advantage.

NAPOLEON HILL

The longer we
dwell on our
misfortunes, the
greater is their
power to harm us.

VOLTAIRE

FORGET THE MISTAKE. REMEMBER THE LESSON

YOU CAN'T WAIT FOR IT – YOU HAVE TO MAKE IT HAPPEN.

Margot Robbie

You just can't beat
the person who
never gives up.

BABE RUTH

FOCUS

ON

YOU

YOU

Make

YOUR OWN

luck.

ERNEST HEMINGWAY

THE DESIRE
ACCOMPLISHED
IS SWEET TO
THE SOUL.

PROVERBS 13:19

I WALK
slowly,
BUT I

never

WALK
backward.

ABRAHAM LINCOLN

IT'S A

BEAUTIFUL

DAY TO DO

HARD

THINGS

The reward of a
thing well done is
to have done it.

RALPH WALDO EMERSON

THE DISTANCE IS NOTHING; IT IS ONLY THE FIRST STEP THAT IS DIFFICULT.

Marquise du Deffand

TAKE CONTROL OF YOUR DESTINY

THERE'S ONLY ONE
CORNER OF THE UNIVERSE
YOU CAN BE CERTAIN OF
IMPROVING, AND THAT'S
YOUR OWN SELF.

ALDOUS HUXLEY

You never
know how the
tough times
you are going
through today will
inspire someone
else tomorrow.

TIM TEBOW

If you **don't go,** you'll NEVER KNOW.

ROBERT DE NIRO

EVERY
MORNING IS
A CHANCE
AT A NEW
DAY

IT'S ALL ABOUT...
manifesting
WHAT YOU WANT IN
your life
WITH THE POWER OF
THOUGHT, WITH THE
POWER OF YOUR MIND
AND YOUR ENERGY.

ALESHA DIXON

Hard work and
ambition can take
you a long way.

DWAYNE JOHNSON

NEVER LET THE HATERS GET YOU DOWN

ALL EXPERIENCE IS AN ARCH TO BUILD UPON.

Henry Adams

The

essence

of life is

going

forward.

AGATHA CHRISTIE

I CAN BE CHANGED
BY WHAT HAPPENS TO
ME. BUT I REFUSE TO
BE REDUCED BY IT.

MAYA ANGELOU

WHY NOT SEE HOW FAR YOU CAN GO?

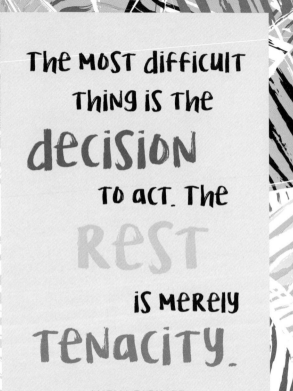

The MOST difficult thing is the DECISION TO act. The REST is MERELY TENACITY.

AMELIA EARHART

WE ALL
start
SOMEWHERE.
IT'S WHERE YOU
end up
THAT COUNTS.

RIHANNA

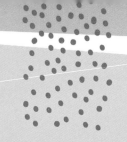

DON'T WAIT FOR
OPPORTUNITY —
CREATE IT

Life changes very quickly, in a positive way, if you let it.

LINDSEY VONN

PEOPLE MAY HEAR YOUR WORDS, BUT THEY FEEL YOUR ATTITUDE.

John C. Maxwell

I learned that
courage
was not the
absence of
fear, but the
triumph
over it.

NELSON MANDELA

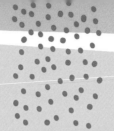

TRUST
YOUR
HEART

TAKE CHANCES, MAKE
MISTAKES. THAT'S
HOW YOU GROW.

MARY TYLER MOORE

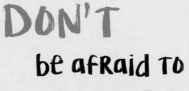

DON'T
be afraid to
PUSH
the
boundaries.

PAULA RADCLIFFE

YOUR

victory

**IS RIGHT AROUND
THE CORNER.**

Never give up.

NICKI MINAJ

Success always
demands a
greater effort.

WINSTON CHURCHILL

EVERY WINNER
HAS SCARS.

Herbert N. Casson

ALL

DARK NIGHTS

EVENTUALLY
LEAD TO

BRIGHTER

DAYS

Accept

who you
are; and
revel in it.

MORRIE SCHWARTZ

VICTORY BELONGS
TO THE MOST
PERSEVERING.

NAPOLEON BONAPARTE

THERE IS —— NOTHING YOU —— CAN'T DO

You learn by
doing
and by
falling
over.

RICHARD BRANSON

WHAT LIES
behind us
AND WHAT LIES
before us
ARE TINY MATTERS
COMPARED TO
WHAT LIES
within us.

HENRY S. HASKINS

I know the sun
will rise in the
morning, that there
is a light at the end
of every tunnel.

MICHAEL MORPURGO

KNOW YOUR OWN WORTH

THE WORLD IS MORE MALLEABLE THAN YOU THINK AND IT'S WAITING FOR YOU TO HAMMER IT INTO SHAPE.

Bono

Being brave
isn't the
absence
of fear. Being
brave is having
that fear but
finding a way
through it.

BEAR GRYLLS

RADIATE
POSITIVITY

POUR YOUR TIME AND
PASSION INTO WHAT BRINGS
YOU THE MOST JOY.

MARIE KONDO

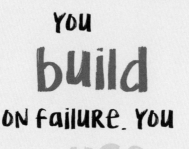

YOU **build** ON FAILURE. YOU use IT AS A STEPPING STONE.

JOHNNY CASH

IF YOU DON'T
GO OUT ON THE
branch,
YOU'RE NEVER
GOING TO GET THE
best fruit.

SARAH PARISH

SET GOALS AND EXCEED THEM

There is no dream
that's too big.

LADY GAGA

DO THE DIFFICULT THINGS WHILE THEY ARE EASY AND DO THE GREAT THINGS WHILE THEY ARE SMALL.

Lao Tzu

DO NOT

YIELD

Great works
are performed,
not by
strength,
but by
perseverance.

SAMUEL JOHNSON

THE ONLY WAY OF
DISCOVERING THE LIMITS
OF THE POSSIBLE IS
TO VENTURE A LITTLE
WAY PAST THEM INTO
THE IMPOSSIBLE.

ARTHUR C. CLARKE

ANY TIME

you fall over,

IT'S JUST

you to

STAND UP

THE NEXT TIME.

JOEL EDGERTON

SET YOUR DIAL TO SMILE

Talent

IS LIKE ELECTRICITY.
WE DON'T UNDERSTAND
ELECTRICITY.
We use it.

MAYA ANGELOU

Do not let what you cannot do interfere with what you can do.

JOHN WOODEN

THE BRAVEST THING YOU CAN BE IS YOURSELF

THE LESSONS LEARNED WHEN I DON'T WIN ONLY STRENGTHEN ME.

Lewis Hamilton

Be kind
to yourself.

MEGHAN, DUCHESS OF SUSSEX

I'M NOT THE ONE TO
SORT OF SIT AND CRY
OVER SPILT MILK. I'M
TOO BUSY LOOKING
FOR THE NEXT COW.

GORDON RAMSAY

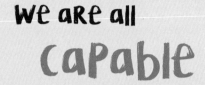

WE ARE ALL
CAPABLE
OF AWAKENING AND
COMMITMENT.
AND BECAUSE
OF THAT,
WE CAN ALL BE
GREAT.

ALEXANDRIA OCASIO-CORTEZ

NEVER EVER

THINK

YOU AREN'T

GOOD ENOUGH

ONE POSITIVE
thought
CAN CHANGE YOUR
whole day.

RUSSELL SIMMONS

If you're interested in finding out more about our books, find us on Facebook at SUMMERSDALE PUBLISHERS and follow us on Twitter at @SUMMERSDALE.

WWW.SUMMERSDALE.COM

Image credits

pp.1, 6, 10, 13, 20, 24, 27, 34, 38, 41, 48, 52, 55, 62, 66, 69, 76, 80, 83, 90, 94, 97, 104, 108, 111, 118, 122, 125, 129, 136, 139, 143, 150, 153, 157, 160 – banners and patterns © Le Chernina/Shutterstock.com

pp.2, 12, 19, 23, 33, 43, 50, 61, 68, 77, 86, 93, 102, 110, 119, 127, 135, 144, 152 © etcberry/Shutterstock.com

pp.9, 16, 29, 39, 51, 57, 65, 74, 82, 89, 98, 107, 116, 124, 133, 141, 149, 158 © Kirsten Hinte/Shutterstock.com